Library Displays

by

Nancy Everhart
Claire Hartz
William Kreiger

The Scarecrow Press, Inc.
Metuchen, N.J., & London
1989

British Library Cataloguing-in-Publication data available

Library of Congress Cataloging-in-Publication Data

Everhart, Nancy.
  Library displays.

  Bibliography: p.
  Includes index.
  1. Library exhibits. I. Hartz, Claire. II. Kreiger,
William. III. Title.
Z717.E9 1989   021.7   88-35640
ISBN 0-8108-2183-4

CONTENTS

PART TWO: OTHER IDEAS

INTRODUCTION

Why library displays? There are many reasons, probably the first being that you have those large glass cases looming at you. However, some others do come to mind. Increased circulation is one. Attractively displaying your library's resources will make patrons more aware of what you have to offer. In doing so, it is hoped that these resources will be checked out. Another reason is to convey a feeling of goodwill to your users. Appropriate displays say you are tuned-in to patron needs, are with the times, and know your collection.

Librarians are busy people and designing displays is in all probability near the bottom of their list of priorities. They also may feel that they "aren't artistic" and stick to decorating their display cases with the same Santa Clauses, hearts, Easter bunnies, Indian corn, and jack-o'-lanterns year after year.

The displays in this book can be created by anyone. Nothing was drawn freehand or constructed without reference pictures or patterns. Common, inexpensive materials and techniques were used. Feel free to follow the directions exactly, or add your own touches.

TYPES OF DISPLAYS

There are basically two types of displays employed in this book and in most libraries. The first type is one where all the books used have a common theme and other materials lend support to this theme. For example, the display on page 42 contains books on rock music and rock stars. Styrofoam heads have Walkman headphones on them whose wires lead to "plug into" the books. Very simply stated, this is a rock music display. Another display, on page 36, embodies a skyline of New York City and books about New York in general and its landmarks. No catchy phrase is needed; the display speaks for itself.

The other type of display illustrated in this book is one where supporting materials are used that have no real connection to books or libraries but are made to do so by adding a catchy phrase or slogan. For example, after a visit to an American Library Association (ALA) convention, many shopping bags were amassed from various publishers. In order to fit them into a display, a sign was added that said "Shop for the Best Resources at the Library." A very inexpensive display was constructed by simply gift-wrapping empty boxes, adding a few books, and the heading "Unwrap an Exciting Time at the Library." Posters may give you these ideas as in the display on page 70. The caption read, "Don't Get Caught in an Information Jungle." Reference books along with an abundance of plants were combined to give a jungle effect.

WHERE TO GET IDEAS FOR DISPLAYS

Student aides, clerks, or volunteers are usually anxious to help in constructing library displays. The stumbling block in most instances is coming up with a good idea. There is a profusion of sources.

First of all, think of displays as a marketing device in your library. Many ideas can be adapted from the advertising industry. Keep to what is currently popular and brainstorm. For example, Pepsi has the advertising slogan "The Choice of a New Generation." Use this heading as the basis for a display, such as "Books--The Choice of a New Generation," or "The Library--The Choice of a New Generation." Use large sheets of poster board and cut out outlines of a soda bottle or can. Cut out a window in the cardboard so that a book placed on a riser may be viewed. Or cut out small pictures of books from publishers' catalogs, place in empty soda bottles, and stick a straw in the top. Key the colors of the display to the red, white, and blue that Pepsi uses. Use the same lettering style for your sign that they use in their advertising. Use your imagination to "go wild" with a theme, and then eliminate those that you do not have the resources to accomplish.

"Miami Vice" is a very popular television show. We took that theme and expanded it to "Library Vice" for one of our displays in this book (see page 10). MTV is viewed by almost all teens. Rely on some of its images in a diplay. Or incorporate popular song titles into display headings such as "Your Wildest Dreams" by the Moody Blues for a display on dream and sleep books.

Professional journals often have articles containing display ideas. The Book Report has devoted entire issues to the subject.

Look closely at the publishers' ads in School Library Journal. Their ideas are very clever and can be adapted to displays. The ad "Hats off from Bradbury Press" could be changed to "Hats off to Books" and displayed with a collection of someone's hats--cowboy, baseball, beret, etc. An ad from Prentice-Hall used the heading "Get into high gear with Prentice-Hall." "Get into high gear with our automotive books" could be used with car-care manuals, tools, and small auto parts. A myriad of these ads are found in the fall and spring book announcement issues.

The covers of School Library Journal and other library journals also can be adjusted to create displays. A back issue had a drawing of a large playing card with the caption "The Odds Favor Reading." Use the same phrase, cover the bottom of your case in green felt, add some real dice or those made from cardboard or foam, a play roulette wheel, and decks of cards either hung from string or spread out. Many catalogs that you would ordinarily consider junk mail from publishers also have these catchy phrases on their covers.

Ads in newspapers and other general magazines also come in handy. An ad for a horseback riding farm used a drawing of a basket full of leaves and a rake with the heading "Take a Break from the Rake." Follow this lead in the fall to create a display with bushel baskets of leaves, a rake, and perhaps leaves hanging or scattered about the bottom of the case. Arrange books on various levels, also surrounded with leaves. The motto "Take a Break from the Rake" fits in very nicely with leisure reading.

When shopping, notice how displays are used to draw you to products. Keep a small notebook handy to jot down these ideas from the pros. Even if you can't afford elaborate displays, the ideas can be adapted to marketing books. Professional displayers also have their own journals and books, and if you are really ambitious you may wish to purchase a few.

GATHERING MATERIALS

What distinguishes a display from a bulletin board is that displays are three-dimensional and bulletin boards are two-dimensional. Most bulletin boards can be constructed almost entirely of paper. However, items of varying texture and size add interest in display cases and must be located.

If you are a school librarian, students are an excellent source for loan of materials. Two hints here: if you use student items, give them credit with a small card placed in the display and begin asking around at least two months in advance. Our display on space was based on "Star Wars" toys loaned by two students. To go out and purchase them would have been prohibitive. Dolls and stuffed animals are ideal for display cases, as are model cars and airplanes. Students collect all types of things and may be willing to arrange them themselves in a display case to which you can add appropriate books. In fact, you may be able to go an entire year just with displays of student material. Use the school bulletin boards, newspaper, and announcements to recruit items for displays. Keep an eye open at student art and science fairs for appropriate projects as another possibility. Most students are flattered to be asked.

Other people in the community may also have collections or hobbies they would be willing to display. Watch for articles on these people in your local newspaper and contact them. Recruit a senior citizen or parent to make things at home needed for displays.

With the popularity of garage sales, various items suitable for displays can be obtained very cheaply. In the music display on page 44, the busts were purchased at a garage sale for $1.00. A ceramic elephant that stood a foot high and cost only 50¢ was used once as the center of a circus display. If the price is right, buy it and think of ways to build a display around it later.

Contact your local merchants for any throwaways from promotions that they may have. You may find a real gold mine here if a large department store is willing to cooperate with you. Again, do not forget to give credit where credit is due.

Scour after-season sales for Christmas, Valentine, Easter, etc., items that are half-price for next year. Save old magazines for cutouts of people or background pictures. If you are ambitious, maintain a picture file so you can locate these pictures immediately. Better yet, give this job to an aide or volunteer.

Also save mailing tubes, sturdy boxes (especially odd-shaped ones), pieces of styrofoam, and styrofoam "peanuts" and "snow" from book shipments. Save maps from National Geographic magazines that can be tied in with displays on countries, genealogy, and foods. Watch for easy-to-make items in women's magazines such as Good Housekeeping, Family Circle, and Woman's Day.

Send for any free items offered in library journals from publishers. Collect free materials from nature such as leaves, branches, dried flowers and weeds, sand, stones, shells, etc.

"Part One" will show you how to construct items you may not be able to purchase, borrow, or find.

PLANNING FOR DISPLAYS

At the end of the school or calendar year, you should make a list of displays for the upcoming year. One display per month is a good rule of thumb, as displays that are changed less frequently become staid, and changing them more often is too much of a hassle. Special events or holidays may show cause for an extra display here or there.

Your list should reflect the display's theme, lettering that will be used, and items and books needed. If a lot of items need to be gathered, it may be a good idea to place that display closer to the end of the list and place those with items you may already have near the beginning. Ideally, it would be nice to have a set of storage shelves where each shelf could be used to place the materials along with a sign and maybe even a picture, sketch, or photocopy of the display idea.

You should also keep a notebook or file to write down ideas for future displays that you have thought about. Remember the advice above on where to get ideas, and if you see one, write it down or photocopy it and place it in the file. Keep display materials together on shelves or in file cabinets, properly labeled.

Once your display is completed, take a picture of it and add notes as to where you got the materials or special instructions. The same display could easily be repeated in three to four years.

PART ONE

DISPLAYS

1. THREE-DIMENSIONAL DISPLAY

MATERIALS

      Oak tag paper
      Glue

This display consists of three-dimensional paper forms. Students from the 3-D art class constructed these forms using patterns and other information found in various paper sculpture books in the library. There are several artists who work in 3-D design, such as M. C. Esher, Henry Moore, and Alexander Calder. A display could be done on any of them.

Objects were constructed with oak tag paper and decorated with paint and/or color construction paper. Several pieces were hung from thin string to achieve the floating-in-space effect.

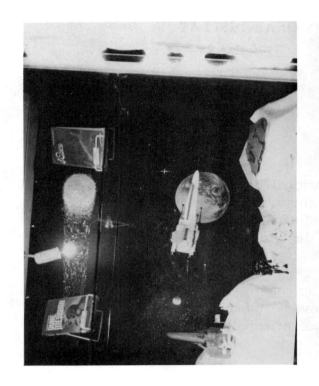 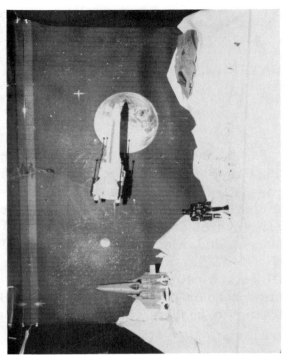

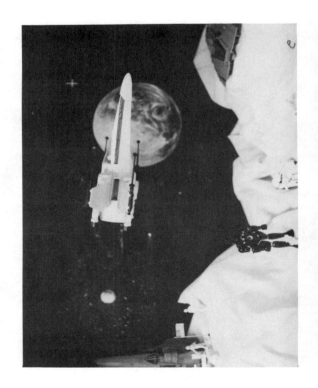 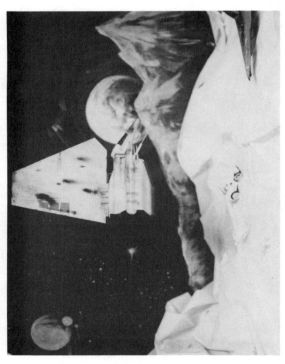

2. SPACE

MATERIALS

> Black cloth, paper, or poster board
> White sheets or carved styrofoam
> Fluorescent paint
> Black light bulbs
> Space toys (brought in by students or made from paper)
> Science fiction books
> Transparent thread
> Sand and pebbles (optional)

The idea behind this display is to make a black background to convey the impression of the emptiness of space. On the black, paintings done in fluorescent paint of planets, comets, moons, stars, and meteors simulate the universe. The effect of stars is accomplished on this background by dipping a toothbrush in the paint, pulling back the bristles, and letting the paint splatter. Mountains drawn at the base are blended with 3-D ones, fashioned very simply by bunching up the white cloth or draping it over empty boxes or other objects to achieve height. The effect to go for is that of an uneven space terrain. An alternative is to use styrofoam cut into uneven layered shapes and glued to form mountains, slopes, and crevices. The paint used here, again, is to highlight peaks and ridges. Students can donate space toys, such as robots, UFOs, "Star Wars" ships, etc. The ships are hung with transparent thread and the other materials are arranged on the shelves in scenes. Books on science fiction or space are used. We used the Dune series which we placed on the top shelves. Black lights replaced the usual bulbs in the cases and that section of the library was darkened for a real attention getter. (Sand and small pebbles can be scattered around to give the effect of a lunar landscape.)

3. CAMINO REAL

MATERIALS

Cardboard Spanish cutouts (purchased)
Sombrero
Statues of Don Quixote and Sancho
Ceramic Spanish vase

The Spanish cardboard cutouts along with the large sombrero were placed in the background. Statues of Don Quixote and Sancho were set on each side of the book Don Quixote. Other books on Spain were placed in this display along with the ceramic vase of Spanish design. This display used materials borrowed from our Spanish instructor. As a goodwill gesture for allowing us to borrow his materials, we gave the cardboard cutouts to the teacher for a bulletin board in his room.

4. TELEVISION

MATERIALS

        Large piece of cardboard
        VCR (real or cardboard)
        VCR tapes
        TV books (with stands)
        Records, magazines
        Magazine covers from TV/video magazines
        Cloth material
        Clear plastic wrap

To create the illusion of watching television while looking into the display case, a large TV frame was constructed from cardboard (see illustration). Inside, a VCR (if you do not have a real one, construct one from a box) was raised by piling books and draping material over them. Arranged among that at different levels are books on television, TV shows and records, along with some VCR tapes. Covers from old video magazines were stapled on the background. Clear plastic was placed over the opening to simulate a screen.

If you offer videotape rental as a library service, you may wish to substitute them in place of the books. Also, books that have been the basis for TV miniseries could be featured.

LIBRARY
VICE
NO EATING
NO TALKING
NO RUNNING
DON'T TAKE
OUT MATERIALS
WITHOUT
CHECK OUT
RESPECT YOUR
FELLOW
STUDENTS

5. LIBRARY VICE

MATERIALS

>Green construction paper
>Plastic flamingos
>"Library Vice" sign
>Pictures of Crockett and Tubbs
>List of library don'ts

Talk about an attention getter! The students loved to stop and look at this one. Central to the display is the "Library Vice" sign, closely imitating the "Miami Vice" logo, down to the exact colors. (The art instructor did it.) Palm tree leaves were cut out of large pieces of green construction paper, stapled together, and fastened to the upper corners of the display case. A list of "library vices"--chewing gum, running, not signing out materials, etc., was hung from fishing line. A backing of pink construction paper, along with photocopies of pictures of "Miami Vice" actors from People magazine gave the sign some sturdiness. Purchased lawn flamingos were placed on either side.

OPTION: Crime books could be used in the display instead of library rules.

6.   SNOOPY--"BOOKS FOR THE DOG DAYS OF SUMMER"

MATERIALS

> Background materials
> Lettering
> Snoopy doll or other stuffed dog with sunglasses
> Wooden dowels
> Striped material
> Sand
> Poster or constructed background scene of a beach

Small beach chairs made from wooden dowels and material hold books in this summer display. Our library Snoopy was added along with the heading "Books for the Dog Days of Summer." A purchased poster fit in nicely, although waves made out of construction paper and a paper sun could do as well. Sand was scattered on the bottom. If you do not feel like making the chairs, get terry cloth and cut out small "beach towels" to place on the sand with books on them. Or place the books in children's sand pails and place a shovel in Snoopy's hand. Any type of books can be used, although fiction seems most appropriate.

"BREEZY" READING
FOR
SPRING BREAK
ROBOTECH
GENESIS
JOHN DALMAS
REGIMENT

7. SPRING--"BREEZY READING"

MATERIALS

        Pedestals
        Cloth material
        Lettering
        Dolls, figurines

A staff member's decanter collection of children in various forms of outdoor play just needed a title to coordinate them with easy-to-read paperbacks. "Breezy Reading for Spring Break" was used because of the balloon and outturned umbrella. Pedestals and boxes added variety to heights and were covered with pastel material, as was the background.

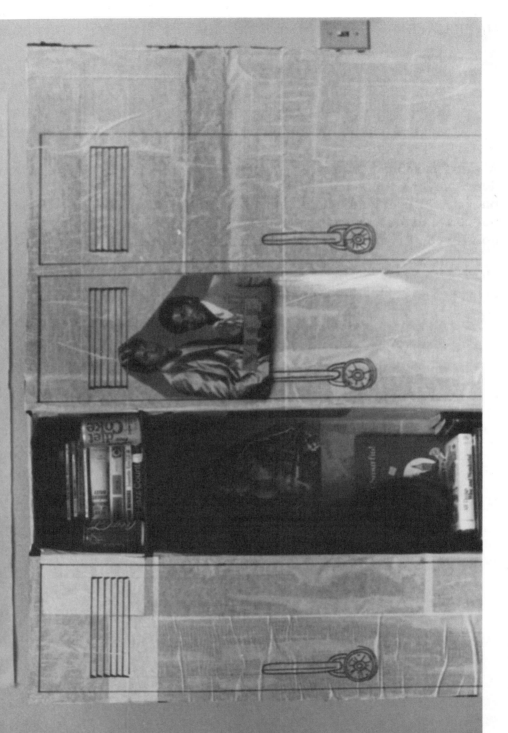

Check for overdue books

8. LOCKER

MATERIALS

> Cardboard
> Paper
> Markers
> Cutouts of popular celebrities
> Soda cans, jacket, notebooks, library books (things found
>   in student lockers)
> Sign

Using a large piece of cardboard, a row of lockers was constructed.
The cardboard was covered with paper and line drawings added to simulate a real locker. The objective of the display was to have students
check their own lockers for overdue books. With this in mind, it was
attempted to make the inside of the cardboard look as realistic as possible with posters, soda cans, folders, backpacks, and books.

9. CAREERS/JOBS

MATERIALS

Classified ad section of newspaper
Career, study books
Office supplies (pencils, pens, stapler, ruler, etc.)

Most items for this display will already be in your library. The idea is to show how you can help patrons in their book search or career planning. The classified section of the newspaper is tacked up to cover the background. Some ads can be circled or checked if desired. Books on study skills, résumé writing, office skills, and careers are arranged with office supplies or aids, such as computer programs, pens, notepads, planners, stamp pads, etc.

Hg
K
As
Si
U
Ce
Ru
Dy
Xe
Zn
Fe
V
CHEMISTRY
PERIODIC TABLE OF THE ELEMENTS
CHEMISTRY
GIANT MOLECULES
GREAT
DISCOVERIES
BY YOUNG
CHEMISTS

10. CHEMISTRY

MATERIALS

       Chemistry beakers
       Flasks, graduated cylinders, etc.
       Molecular models
       Periodic table of elements
       Food coloring and water

SCIENCE WEEK OR SCIENCE FAIR DISPLAY

Borrow what you can from your chemistry department for this display. The beakers and other containers were filled with water and drops of food coloring were added to make the display more colorful. The molecular models were also borrowed from the chemistry department and assembled to resemble molecular formulas. Place an enlarged periodic table on the background and fill in with various chemical symbols. Books on chemistry were placed at various levels to complete this display.

11.   SHOPPING FOR INFORMATION

MATERIALS

    Shopping bags

While at the ALA convention in 1986, we picked up many shopping bags.
The entire display area was filled with bags. Various books, paperbacks,
or computer programs were placed in as suggestions as to what these
shopping bags could hold. A sign was printed from the computer program Print Shop with this slogan: "Shop at Your Library for the Best
Sources." This was mounted on a colored piece of construction paper
and mounted on one of the shopping bags.

SUGGESTIONS: "Information Shopping--Use Your Library"
                  "Shop at Your Library for Free Information"
                  "Fill Your Shopping Bags with Information"
                  "Check Out the Library for Your Best Bargains"

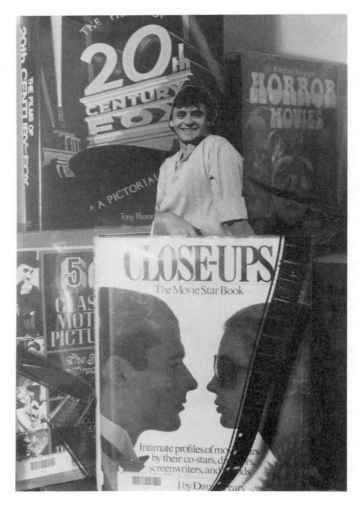

12. MOVIES

MATERIALS

        Cardboard (to make marquee)
        Press-on letters
        Movie reels
        Old filmstrips or films
        Magazine photos of movie stars
        Movie books

A movie marquee was constructed for the top of this display using cardboard covered with paper (see illustration). Press-on letters made the sign "Now Playing at Your School Library" (or a sign of your choice). A large selection of movie books was arranged in the case, standing one on top of the other. To fill in empty spaces, pictures of movie stars were cut from magazines, mounted on cardboard, and stood up with stands (see illustration). Also old filmstrips were draped around the books. Some reels from movie projectors also filled in. Books that have been made into movies could be your heading on the marquee and those books used.

13. HEMINGWAY/SEA

MATERIALS

> Statue or large mounted photograph of Ernest Hemingway
> Netting
> Shells
> Cloth material
> Sea creatures (paper or real)
> Large drawing of fish
> Small treasure chest (optional)

A bust of Ernest Hemingway from Gale Research, sea shells, and netting were purchased items here. (The bust of Ernest Hemingway was purchased by a library patron in memory of a family member and donated to our library; thus the cost of the statue was not taken from library funds for this display.) If you do not have a bust, mount a picture or photocopy of one. The large fish is "blown up" from the overhead projector. Shells from my son's collection filled in, as did a small treasure chest. Hemingway's <u>The Old Man and the Sea</u> was also included.

Another display was created by using the same items and replacing the Hemingway materials with additional large shells, paper honeycomb fish, and books.

If you wanted a different background for the sea display, you could hang book jackets from threads to look like a school of fish, or use the small cutouts (taken from various book catalogs). You could also put paper fins on the jackets or make fish and glue the small pictures of books on them.

TWAS THE NIGHT

BEFORE CHRISTMAS AND ALL

THRU THE HOUSE

A Book of Christmas

14. CHRISTMAS

MATERIALS

> Candle houses (or other houses)
> Christmas books or mounted poem (" 'Twas the Night Before
> Christmas")
> Lettering
> Small trees
> Santa and reindeer (purchased cardboard)
> Snowflakes (purchased or made from paper)

A closeout sale by one of the classes got us this collection of candle houses to use in a display. What to do? Tie it into Christmas with the slogan " 'Twas the Night Before Christmas and All Through the House." Add a cardboard Santa and reindeer, a few Christmas books--and voila! If you do not want to take your Christmas books out of circulation for the holidays, mount the classic poem "A Visit from St. Nicholas" by Clement Moore and stand it in the display.

ALTERNATE: Straw stars. A bunch of straws can be tied tightly together to make a star. Cut the straws at various lengths to make different size stars. Spray with glitter spray. A dark background could be used in the display and the stars hung at various levels. On the dark background, Santa and his reindeer could be placed. A display light focused on the stars make them glitter to give it a "night" effect.

SUGGESTIONS: Cut out pictures from catalogs, such as the small pictures we used in the Valentine display, and use as tree ornaments. This theme can be used as a tabletop display.

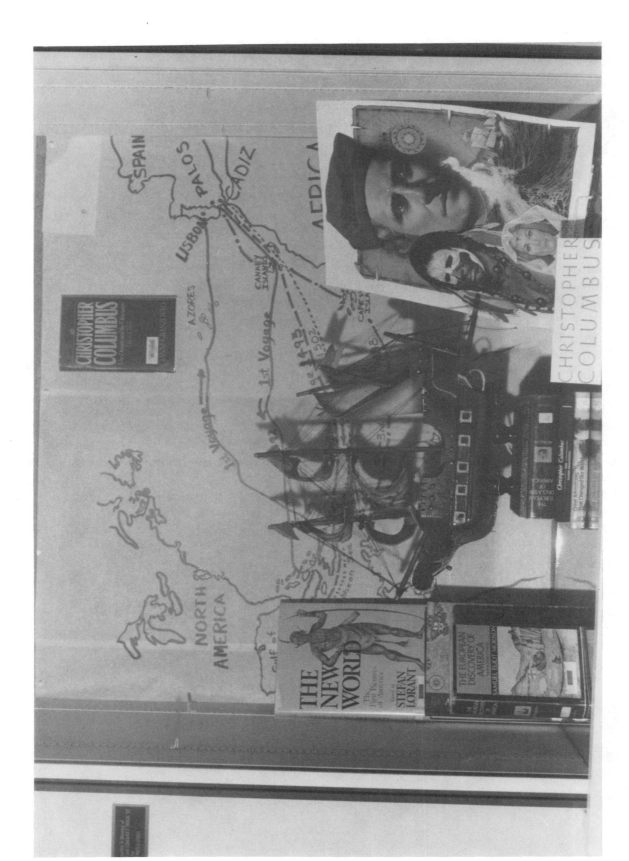

15. CHRISTOPHER COLUMBUS

MATERIALS

> Large sheet of paper (for background)
> Christopher Columbus poster (or picture)
> Ship
> Books on Columbus, discovery of America, etc.

A borrowed sailing ship from one of the office staff (resembling one of the ships used by Columbus) forms the center of this display. If you are fortunate, you may be able to get your hands on models of all three ships. The background is a hand-drawn map taken from an illustration that was enlarged on an overhead or could be done freehand. It depicts the three voyages of Columbus. The corner poster was a "freebie" received when the miniseries Christopher Columbus was about to air on television. We cut off the advertising and also "Christopher Columbus," mounted both on oak tag and stood them up. The books were arranged in the bare spots. The cover from Gianni Granzotto's Christopher Columbus: The Dream and the Obsession hung over a bare spot in the map.

Any type of old map showing the route of Columbus could also be used. Perhaps show a flat planet with one of the ships going off the edge. (This could be a box or a flat piece of cardboard.)

SUGGESTIONS: "Travels of Christopher Columbus"
              "The Voyages of Christopher Columbus"
              "Sail with Christopher"

16. GIFT WRAP--"UNWRAP AN EXCITING TIME AT YOUR LIBRARY"

MATERIALS

        Wrapping paper
        Ribbon
        Tissue paper
        Various sizes of boxes
        Books
        Pin-up lettering
        Pins

This display is also very inexpensive. The only purchased items were the gift wrap and ribbon. Various boxes were colorfully wrapped and arranged with books. Depending on the size of your cases, more or less may be used. The boxes hanging next to the lettering were fastened with large straight pins. Ribbon was curled with scissors and used to fill in bare spots. Some tissue paper sticks out of one of the boxes. This display could also be a Christmas one, with gift book suggestions in the display.

17. SUN

MATERIALS

       Yellow construction paper
       Yellow and orange crepe paper
       Book jackets
       Tape, markers, fishing line

Make a round face for the sun on yellow construction paper. Secure it with fishing line on top and bottom. Twist the crepe paper to form rays. Tape or staple the sides to the case. Hang book jackets on thread around rays. Write a slogan on the crepe paper.

SUGGESTIONS: "Sizzling Summer Reading"
                "The Heat Is On!"
                "Sunny Books"
                "Catch Some Rays with Books"
                "Lie Under the Sun with a Book"

Another suggestion for this display is to put sunglasses on the books that are standing up.

18. NEW YORK

MATERIALS

      Enlarging photocopier
      Paper signs
      Heavy wire

All you need for this display is paper! The idea came from an ad in the New York Times Magazine. The line drawing in the ad section is of New York's Central Park and surrounding buildings. This was cut evenly into eight parts, enlarged on the photocopier, and pasted back together to the size of the background of our display cases. Some sections were copied twice, pasted to a box, and placed in front of the same section to give a three-dimensional effect. Signs of the various New York landmarks and streets made on the computer Print Shop program were pasted on wire of various lengths and mixed in among the books on New York.

This display could also be adapted to other New York themes such as "The Big Apple," where you could cut out apples out of red and green construction paper or purchase plastic apples and place them randomly in the display case among the books or hang from transparent string from the top of the display.

19. DISNEY

MATERIALS

The "Read" poster from ALA with Mickey Mouse
Borrowed stuffed animals and figurines
Life magazine
Art and Man magazine
Book stand

Disney characters are always attention getters. Mickey reading a book
was a poster available from ALA which was expanded upon by adding
stuffed and ceramic figures. Depending on what and how many characters
you have, they can be arranged in any number of ways with books. The
books chosen here deal with Walt Disney and Walt Disney World but they
do not necessarily have to.

OTHER POSSIBILITIES: Disney Computer Software/Filmstrips. Have a
contest where kids bring in animals and their fellow students guess to
whom they belong. Or teachers name their favorite Disney character and
students guess which teacher likes which character. You could also construct a three-dimensional Cinderella castle or staple outline of one to
the background or tape on glass and look through the door. The title
might be "Enter the Magic Kingdom of Reading." Disney cutouts can be
made from cardboard, used with the overhead and/or opaque projectors.

20. VIETNAM

MATERIALS

        Camouflage cloth material
        Army paraphernalia (backpack, canteen, books, helmets,
           dog tags, shirts--whatever is available)
        Books on Vietnam
        Lettering
        Toy or paper machine gun

Time-Life recently put out a series of books called "The Vietnam Experience." Their promotional envelope-flyer had a camouflage background which we expanded upon for this display. We also used their idea of the stencil-like lettering.

Tack the material on the background and then affix the lettering. We used a drawing of a machine gun, but a realistic toy could be used. Arrange the books on Vietnam with whatever you can scrape up from students and faculty. Use leftover cloth materials to cover books or platforms on which to place the books. (Although we used helmets, a backpack, and a canteen, any paraphernalia could be used.)

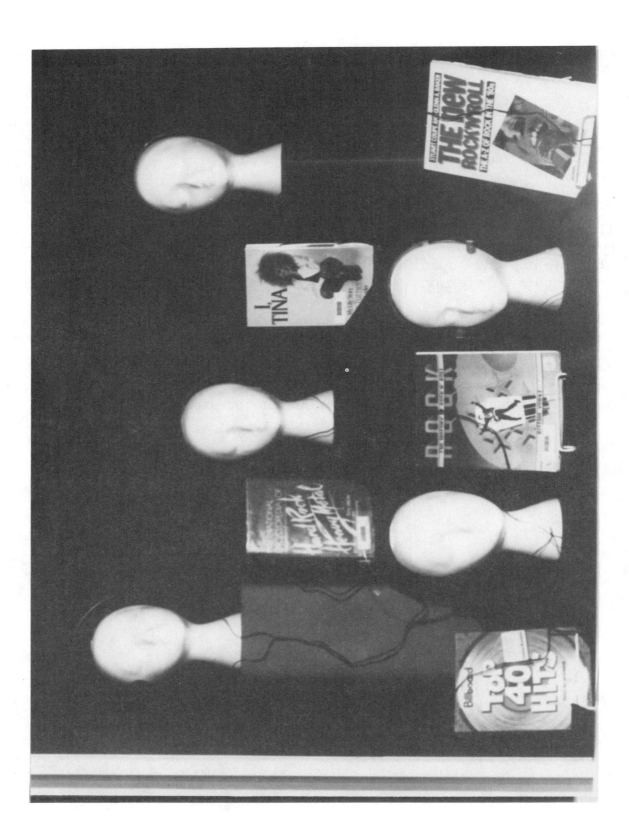

21. ROCK MUSIC

MATERIALS

        Black paper or material
        Styrofoam heads (purchased at a local department store
           for $2)
        "Walkman" headphones
        Rock music books, biographies of rock stars, records

Place heads on various levels. Place headphones on head, leading wires to plug into books. Black lights may be used. Earphones can be made from paper, cardboard, foam, felt, etc. Cord could be represented with strings, yarn, etc. This display has the greatest potential for student interest.

22. MUSIC

MATERIALS

        Sheet music
        Statues of musicians
        Construction paper

This display was very inexpensive to construct. The background of sheet
music gives it a different touch. Musical symbols were cut from black
and gold construction paper and placed randomly on the sheet music.
The statues were purchased at a garage sale for 75¢ for the pair. Books
on music were placed to complete the display. If you do not have statues,
musical instruments could be used in this display, in the form of musical
instruments floating (or on notes).

23. SCARECROW

MATERIALS

>Straw
>Plastic lettering
>Scarecrows
>Corn husks
>Pumpkins (plastic or real)
>Black cloth or black construction paper
>Orange construction paper

Black material was hung to form a background. A quarter moon was cut from orange construction paper and placed in the upper right-hand corner of the background. (A full moon or half moon could also be used.) Plastic letters were used to make the slogan. If you do not have plastic lettering, you could make the letters from construction paper. Straw was spread over the shelf and also used to form a mound to make a haystack. (The straw was saved from a shipment of books.) Pumpkins were placed at the base of the haystack along with a small scarecrow. If you are artistically inclined, a scarecrow could be easily made with the use of a dowel, some scraps of material, a round styrofoam ball for the head, and your imagination.

Real cornstalks could be used and the theme changed to a Halloween display.

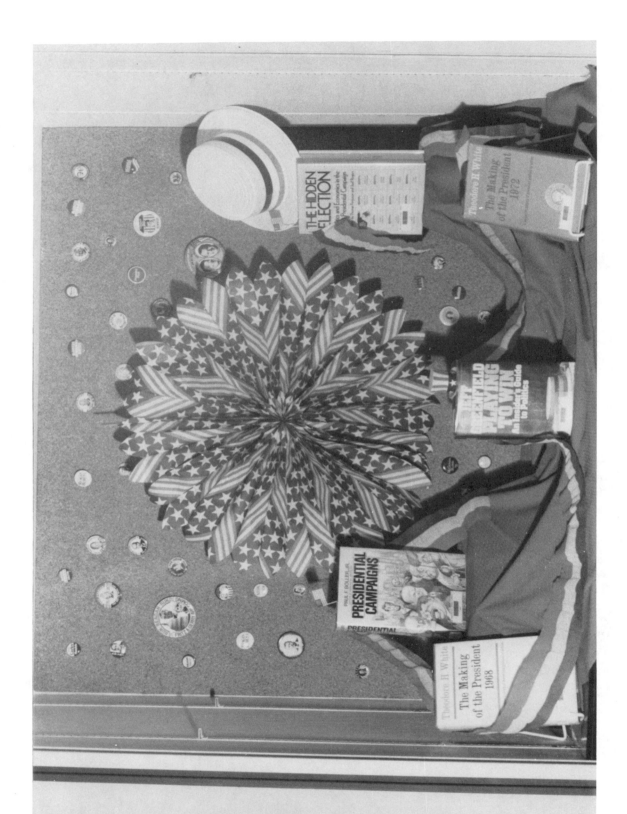

24. ELECTION

MATERIALS

   Red cloth
   Book stands
   Red, white, and blue crepe paper
   Election hats
   Cocktail toothpick flags (purchased)
   Red, white, and blue tissue paper decoration
   Election buttons
   Party novelty hats (purchased)

Election books and the colors red, white, and blue are the focus of this display. First, a base was constructed with various books and boxes used to create varying heights. A red cloth was placed over this. Election books were arranged by opening to stand them up and using book stands. After the books were arranged, red, white, and blue crepe paper was draped among and around them. Small cocktail toothpick flags were stuck in the books. Also, a small "Uncle Sam" hat was placed on one of the books, as was a plastic "straw" election hat. The hanging flag ornament was also purchased. A collection of campaign buttons from one of our faculty was pinned up in the background for a finishing touch. No slogan was used as the common theme of election books speaks for itself.

25. CATS

MATERIALS

> Cat stick-up (from Upstart--<u>see</u> "Sources")
> "PURRRRR" lettering

A quickie display using purchased materials from Upstart. Although intended as signs, with a little ingenuity and tape, the cats with the Dewey divisions signs on them can be made to stand up. Match a book from each Dewey division to the sign. A large "PURRRRR" sign was added to coordinate the display.

VARIATIONS: "Don't Be CAT-atonic--READ!"
              "PURRRRRfect Books"
              "Books Are the CAT's Meow"

Have students bring in stuffed cats, collections. Put paper cat ears, and pipe cleaner whiskers on books to look like a cat.

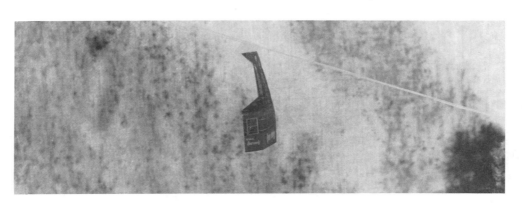

26. SKIING

MATERIALS

        Cloth backdrop
        "Snow" materials
        Rocks, small plastic deer, plastic trees, and bushes
        Homemade ski lodge
        "Fake" snow (or confectionary sugar)
        Skiing books or old skiing magazines or brochures
        Odd pieces of styrofoam
        Thread
        Lettering

OPTIONAL: Fake snowman
           Small skating scene
           Popsicle sticks cut like skis sticking out of the snow

A most popular display that cost next to nothing to make. The larger your display cases, the more lifts, slopes, and skiers you can add. White cloth formed the background on which mountains and trees were drawn with chalk. A slope was constructed with odd styrofoam pieces over which snow-like cotton (found in stores around Christmas time) was draped. At different times, we have used skiers from a mobile or ones that have been cut out of old skiing magazines, mounted on cardboard, and pinned in place on the slopes. The effect is very real and the students loved it. A ski lodge was drawn on the front of a triangular box. Again, cardboard skiers were placed standing and walking around it. A ski lift was constructed by stringing thread from the bottom of the display case to the top of the slope. Pictures of ski lifts were found in skiing magazines, mounted on cardboard, and glued to the string. Skiing books and magazines were added as were plastic deer, rocks, and plastic evergreen trees and bushes to fill in. If desired, skis could be cut out of popsicle sticks and stuck in styrofoam snow banks around the lodge. The title "Books on Skiing" was formed by following the outline of one of the mountains in the background. Snow was placed around after everything was in place.

SUGGESTIONS: "It's All Downhill After Reading Our Books"
              "Downhill Reading"
              "Powder-Packed Books"
              "It's Snow Secret"

27. WILD WEST

MATERIALS

    Cloth background
    Put-together town (Dover cardboard houses--see "Sources")
    Miniature gunfighters (lead figures)
    Sand for gound
    Book jackets (wild West, famous gunfighters)
    Rope

The same cardboard town used in a Christmas scene was recycled to form a Western town. Small figures of cowboys were purchased and arranged among them. Sand covered the bottom to form a surface. A free poster obtained at a convention, "Cowboys of the Wild West," gave us the original idea. Book jackets on the wild West, its history, and its people were added. The lettering was done by stapling rope on a handwritten slogan.

SUGGESTIONS: "Outlaws Are IN at the Library"
               "Outlaws Are in 978 (and 921)"
               "Rope Yourself a Good Book About the West"

Another suggestion for this display: Put cowboy hats on the books-- black for the bad buys, white for the good guys. Handkerchief masks can be placed around the books or sheriff's badges made from construction paper can be placed on the books.

28. UNICORNS

MATERIALS

> Unicorns (stuffed, ceramic figures, etc.)
> Cloth for background and floor
> Books on unicorns, mythology
> Unicorn poster

Show off a faculty member's or student's collection in your library's cases. Our English teacher collects unicorns and loaned them to us for this display. A solid black background was used which really sets them off. A unicorn poster was purchased and books on mythology added. Luckily, we had two copies of The Lore of the Unicorn which fit in nicely. That gave us the idea of making this display symmetrical, with nearly the same items on both sides.

Many people collect animal figures--frogs, bears, elephants, etc. These make very appealing and stimulating displays for young people. They are also very easy to put together! Usually all that is needed are stands or boxes to achieve various heights.

If you are borrowing someone's personal items for a display, be sure to place a card in the case giving that person recognition. You may get more volunteers that way!

THE LIBRARY IS THE PLACE TO BEE...

FLOWERS FOR LILLI

THE BUMBLEBEE FLIES ANYWAY

29. THE LIBRARY IS THE PLACE TO BEE...

MATERIALS

> Background paper or material
> Lettering
> Honeycomb tissue paper bees
> Honeycomb tissue paper flower pots
> Books, book stands

This display is a quickie done entirely with purchased materials. The idea came from a billboard about a bank that was "the place to bee...." The Bumblebee Flies Anyway by Robert Cormier and Flowers for Lillian by Anna Gilbert were used because the titles fit the display. You could also use your insect or flower books in this display.

SUGGESTIONS: "Stay as Busy as a Bee in the Library"
"Bee Informed--Use Your Library"
"Make a Bee-Line to Your Library"

Another idea would be to fill entire background of display with flat flowers and have bees sitting on them. Or create a honeycomb design using egg cartons (the gray papier-mâché ones that eggs sometimes come in) and have bees sitting among the honeycombs. Also a beehive can be made from these egg cartons. This can be hung in the display or from a branch.

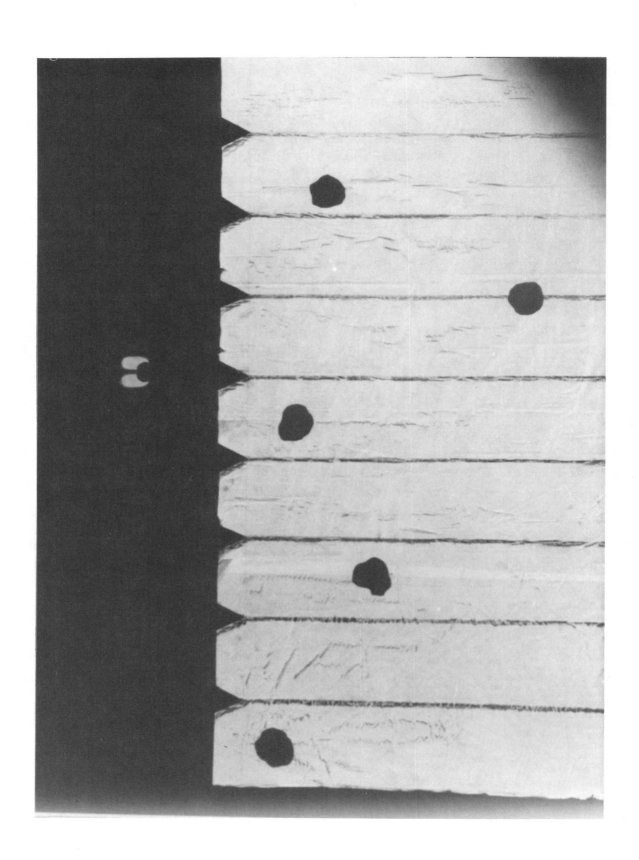

30. PEEK-THROUGH FENCE

MATERIALS

        Cardboard
        Markers

A fence was constructed from a large piece of cardboard and detailed with color markers. Holes were cut out so that the student could peep in. Behind the fence, you can put a variety of books such as bestsellers, sports, etc.--anything that would draw student interest. A pair of eyes were drawn on paper, cut out, and put in the background area.

SUGGESTIONS: "Take a Closer Look"
              "Well Worth Peeking"

31. VALENTINE

MATERIALS

> Large pieces of cardboard to make Valentine candy box
> Small cupcake papers
> Lace
> Netting

Netting was used to fill in the entire display case on which the large Valentine candy box was set. Pictures of books were cut from various old book catalogs and placed inside the paper cupcake holders to simulate pieces of candy. The cupcake holders were then glued inside the Valentine. The theme, here again, is self-explanatory. Strings of white lights could also be placed under the netting.

SUGGESTIONS: "How Sweet It Is"--Reading
"This Valentine Is for 'Readers' Instead of 'Eaters' "

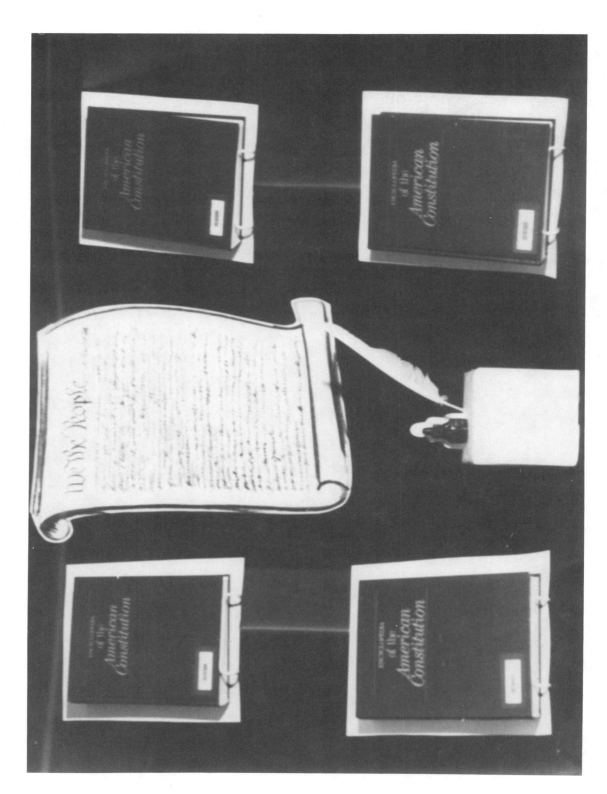

32. CONSTITUTION

MATERIALS

> White construction paper
> Quill pen or feather to resemble a pen
> Inkwell
> Book stands
> Color cloth for background (optional)

The Constitution scroll was drawn on white construction paper and the text was done in calligraphy. Instead of a clutter of books we decided to focus on The Encyclopedia of the American Constitution four-volume set. All that needed to be added were a quill pen and inkwell. Again, this display loudly presents its theme. It is very simple and takes little time to complete.

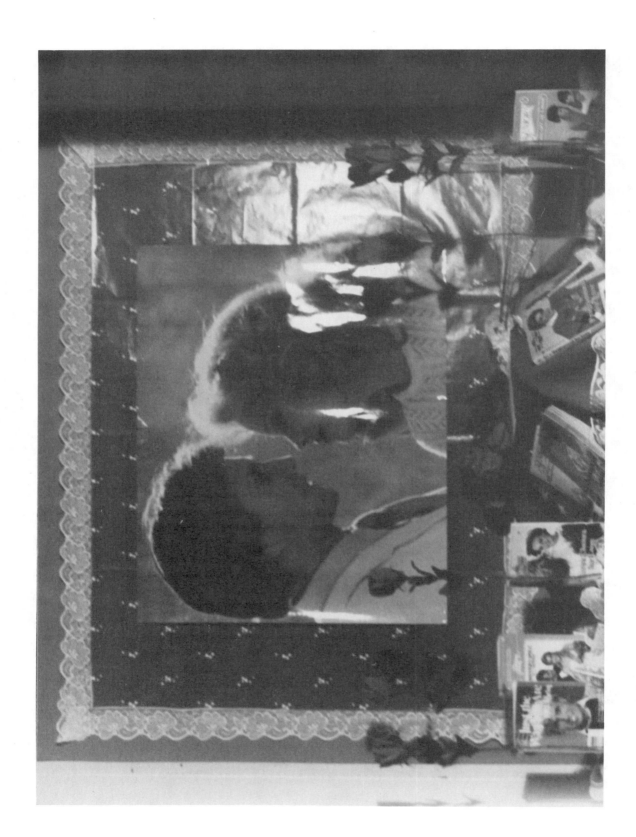

33. LOVE

MATERIALS

       Poster
       Wrapping paper with hearts on it
       Lace
       Roses, real or fabric
       Vases
       Paperbacks

The poster, wrapping paper, and lace were used as the background which shows the theme of this display--love, romance, valentines, etc. Vases with artificial or real rosebuds were placed randomly among the paperbacks. We picked the paperbacks whose titles suggested love and romance. Lace was also placed in and around the paperbacks to create this eye-catching display. The only cost of this display was the wrapping paper. All other items were borrowed or reused from other displays.

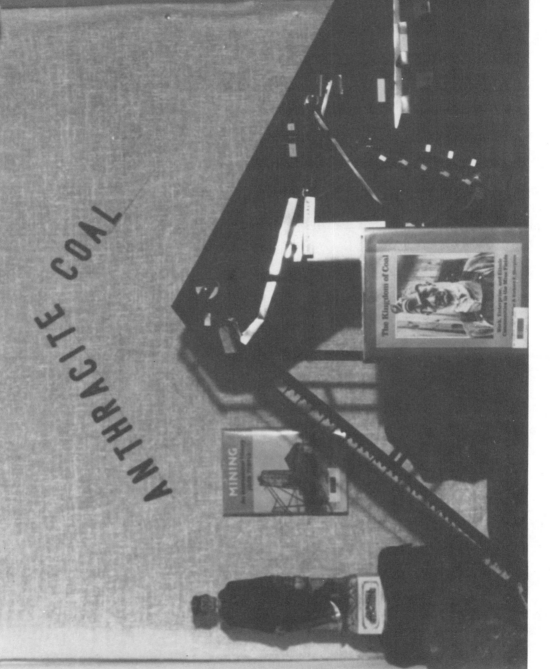

34. COAL

MATERIALS

       Statue of a miner (borrowed)
       Coal breaker (from student project)
       Lumps and pieces of coal
       Books: <u>The Kingdom of Coal</u> and <u>Mining</u>

Being located in the heart of a coal mining area, this was a very simple display to construct. The scaled model of the breaker, built by a student for a history project, was donated to our library. The miner and the lumps of coal were placed in the display along with the two books on anthracite coal and mining. Black lettering was placed on the white background.

SUGGESTIONS: A background could be drawn showing the silt banks that are synonymous with the mining areas.

35. INFORMATION JUNGLE

MATERIALS

Wood blocks
Green plants (plastic or real)
Poster

Wooden blocks of various heights were placed to use as stands to hold "information" books. The green plants were placed in the case to fill in and give the appearance of a jungle. The poster "Trapped" was used for the background.

SUGGESTION: Animals such as a lion or a monkey can also be used here sitting on a book or among the plants.

36. WEDDING

MATERIALS

> Cloth or construction paper for the background
> Lace
> Satin ribbon in various widths, color coordinated to match
>   the background
> Bridal dolls (Avon was used in this display)
> Flowers
> Small steel posts
> Paper wedding bells

The solid color background used in this display was for contrast. Tiers were formed on which the bridal dolls were placed on a wider satin ribbon. The narrow, white satin ribbon was tied into bows with 6-inch spacing between the bows and attached to the steel posts to simulate the side aisle of a church. Flowers were placed on top of the tiers to add some color. An arch was formed for the background with netting and lace. The book Bride's Book of Etiquette was placed on a higher setting to display the theme of the book.

SUGGESTIONS: "The Perfect Marriage--Books and Students"
                  "The Perfect Marriage--Libraries and Students"

37. STAGE

MATERIALS

> Satin material
> Cardboard
> Shakespeare books
> Paper faces of comedy and tragedy
> Enlarged figurines of Shakespeare (taken from <u>Model Theatres</u>
> book, or could be taken from a coloring book or hand
> drawn)

Satin material was stapled and gathered on the back wall to resemble a theatre curtain. If you do not want to take the time to simulate a theatre curtain, you could use a tension drapery rod and any drapery you may have. A collection of miniature Shakespeare books was arranged as the stage. Once again, our enlarging copier was utilized to blow up the Shakespearean figures which were colored in with markers and pencils. Comedy and tragedy faces were drawn freehand and pasted on the curtain to fill in.

This display could have many variations. General theatre books could be used--not just Shakespeare--along with someone's collection of playbills. For other alternates, such as an opera display, use opera glasses, records, pictures of famous opera stars, etc. This same display could also be changed to a ballet scene. Instead of paper figures, use dolls of wood or plastic, if available. You can also purchase the cutout doll books from Dover or Belleprohon and use these in any movie, ballet, opera, play, etc., scenes.

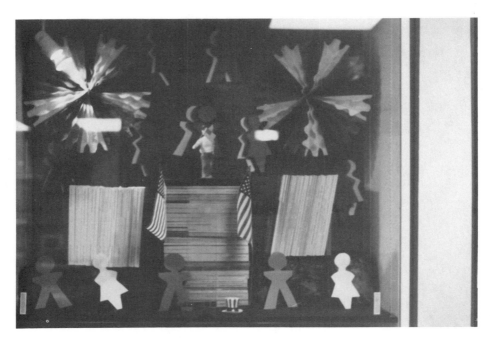

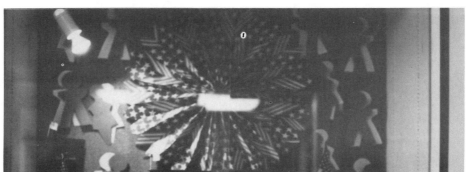

38. CENSUS OR POPULATION

MATERIALS

> Construction paper
> Small American flags (optional)
> Tissue decorations (optional)

A display on census, population, or statistics books can be made very simply and colorfully. Outline figures of a man and a woman were made as a pattern from which a large number of similar "people" were cut. (The pattern was taken from the symbols on our rest room doors.) If the books deal only with the United States, you may wish to use red, white, and blue for the people, even layering them on top of each other. Flags and/or other purchased "stars and stripes" materials are inexpensive additions. Or, if the books deal with world statistics, coordinate the colors of the figures to those of the book jackets.

The more paper cutouts the better in this display. Place them on the background, on the books, and standing everywhere in the case.

39. PRESIDENTS

MATERIALS

       Portraits from Oltenheimer Publishers, Inc.
       Cardboard eagle/flag
       Coins from Treasury Bureau of the Mint
       Red, white, and blue cloth or construction paper

A collection of presidential coins and portraits forms the basis of this display. Three levels were made in red, white, and blue cloth or construction paper. Beard's The Presidents in American History was placed in the case, but any books on presidents would do.

On the background, the portraits of the most recent presidents were used along with the colorful cardboard eagle. The collection of presidential coins was donated to the library and is used in many of our displays, especially in the month of February. This is a very simple display to do and the use of the red, white, and blue cloth makes it very eye-catching.

PART TWO

OTHER IDEAS

ONE-COLOR DISPLAY

Coordinate the display by focusing on one color. Pick out books that all have the same color cover and display with items of that color. For example, use all green books with St. Patrick's Day items or all yellow books with silk daffodils.

NATURAL DISPLAY

Stand books on pieces of burlap material. In between the books lay dried flowers, weeds that you can gather from the outdoors or purchased dried baby's breath. The idea here is to keep the surroundings very bland to show off the attractiveness of the books themselves. This is a good display when you have many shelves to fill.

GRADUATION

Salute your seniors as graduation approaches: mount photos of the senior class (group or individual, depending on school size). If you use individual photos, place a college catalog, career book, or actual item relative to the career. To fill in the display, make diplomas by rolling up white paper and tying with a ribbon. Make graduation hats out of construction paper and attach yarn tassels. Place yearbooks in if more items are needed.

PROM

Show how the library can aid students in preparing for the prom. Include books on makeup, construction of clothing, and dating. Open Seventeen magazines to ads for prom gowns and tuxedos. Use the theme "Prom Planning Begins in the Library." Arrange the books with Barbie dolls dressed in gowns.

RAINBOW

Make a large rainbow for a backdrop and use the title "You Can Read Every Color of the Rainbow" for this display. Get books that have a color in their title, such as The Color Purple and The Greening of America, and place in the case. Hang paper rainbows from the top of the case among the books.

FACULTY BABY PICTURES

Get faculty to give you a childhood picture and the title of their favorite

book at that age. Try to get that book and place it with the picture.
If you cannot get the actual book, make a sign with the title on it to
stand by the picture. Make the display into a contest where students
try to guess the faculty member. Number the pictures and have a contest sheet near the display or at the checkout desk for those who wish
to participate. A variation of the baby picture idea is to have faculty
write a few sentences of how books or a certain book influenced their
lives and display this information.

BALLOON

A very simple display idea is to purchase a package of library promotion
balloons from Upstart Co. (see "Sources"). Place books in the case and
fill the rest of the case with the balloons. Use regular air to fill the
balloons, as helium will deflate in a day. In the center you can place a
book suspended from the top or placed on a pedestal. A contest can also
be used in this display to guess how many balloons fill the display case.

FILM LOOP OR VIDEOTAPE

Remember the old 8-mm film loops and projectors? Many are no longer
used by schools but can be adapted to a display. Have the projector
running the film loop in the display case and arrange books that deal
with that subject around it (usually these are how-to tapes). If your
case is large, use several projectors. The same idea can be used with
video cassette recorder and television, but must be monitored. The film
loop projector runs continuously and is usually only a few minutes in
length.

CRATE

Get wooden crates used to pack fruit from a grocery store. Place posters
that promote books on the bottoms and stand the crates up both horizon-
tally and vertically. Also place some on top of each other, alongside,
etc. Put some books on the crates. Fill in bare spots with shavings
and sawdust. Or show a crate filled with books and use the slogan "New
Books Have Arrived."

MARDI GRAS

Hang streamers from the top of the case and among books on New Orleans,
Mardi Gras, etc. Crumple up colorful tissue paper into balls and arrange

with the books. Throw confetti on the completed display. The idea here is to make the display as colorful as possible. This display could also be adapted for a New Year's display.

SUMMER

Take a piece of string and fasten it on an angle from the upper left to lower right of the display case. Make triangular flags in red, yellow, and blue and hang them on the string, pointing downward. Get different sized balls and paint them in red, blue, and yellow also. Arrange with books for a summery, nautical display. Also books on summer activities could be added for a change.

GRASSY DISPLAY

There are several possibilities here. First, you could get a large Easter basket, line it with foil, place soil in, and plant grass seeds. After the grass grows, put eggs in it for use in an Easter display. Or plant the grass on a large flat surface such as a cookie sheet. Place a tee with a golf ball on it for a display with golfing books and magazines. The grass on the cookie sheet could also be used with figures of cows or other farm animals for a farming display.

DAVID LETTERMAN

Get a cutout, or blow up a picture of David Letterman and construct a "Museum of the Hard to Believe" like he has on his show. Some things that could be placed in it are write-ups of unusual things that have happened in the library, strange reference questions, books with notes on them such as "Never checked out by ...," or "Has all of the answers to the biology test," or "Has the power to keep you awake at night," etc. Cutouts of people who appear frequently on Letterman could also be added. Again, this is another great student-interest display.

STATE

Put a large map of your state as the background of this display. Have pieces of yarn or string radiating from towns or cities on the map to actual products of that area that are in the display case. Fill in with state books.

HOW A BOOK IS MADE

Write to or visit a publisher and ask for a book in several stages of production. Display as a step-by-step process with explanations of each step.

SEASONS

Cut out large cardboard letters (about 12 inches high) with the word "spring" (or summer, fall, or winter). Stand them up in the display case by leaning them against a long box or stacks of books. Display books so that they appear to be standing on top of each letter.

SPRING: Hang kites, arrange paper flowers, construct a tree, and have a large doll or mannequin leaning against it reading a book.

SUMMER: Spread sand on the bottom of the display case, arrange buckets and shovels with the books, or place books on small "beach towels."

FALL: Gather acorns in the fall and place on the bottom of the display with the theme "Out of Little Acorns Big Oak Trees Grow." Tie it in with the idea that "Out of Knowledge Successful People Grow--Use Your Library." Also use the theme "Don't Fall Behind." Collect some leaves and spread them on the background and on the bottom of the display area ("Gather Your Knowledge Before You Fall Behind").

WINTER: Spray branches with fake snow or white paint. Hang paper snowflakes. Add white Christmas lights if available. Or make sleds out of popsicle sticks and have them sticking out of snow banks.

COZY READING SCENE

Pretend the glass front of the display case is the window of someone's home. Use masking tape to construct fake window panes if you like. Spray the glass with spray snow. Inside, use a doll or mannequin sitting in a cozy chair by a fireplace reading a book. Or have the doll in bed with a cozy quilt also reading a book. Make the scene as cozy as possible.

BUSINESS AND INDUSTRY

Invite local companies to display their products. Display with books on business, entrepreneurship, etc.

NOSE

Buy some of those "funny" glasses with noses and mustaches on them and attach to books. Use with the heading "The Students Who Know Everything Have Their Noses in a Book."

CLASSICS

Display classic books with other "classics" such as a single rose in a vase, Wedgwood china, a small Oriental rug, a model of a Rolls Royce, etc.

CHRISTMAS

ELVES: Make your own elves or buy them. Buy Christmas garland. Stand books in the display case and arrange the elves so it looks like they are draping garland over and among the books.

STOCKINGS: Tack paper that looks like bricks (available at Christmas time) on the back of the display case. Hang small Christmas stockings on the outer edges of display case shelves. Arrange books on the shelves.

"BOOK I WANT FOR CHRISTMAS": Survey teachers as to what book they want for Christmas. Make a sign with their name and the book title on it. Place on wrapped package under a small Christmas tree.

BUILDING BLOCKS

Take boxes and paint them to look like large building blocks. Display with the heading "Building Blocks of Knowledge" or "Building Blocks of Research" and display with reference books.

PUZZLE

With the heading "Puzzled? We Have the Answers" arrange books with jigsaw puzzle pieces. Make the lettering look like puzzle pieces.

UNLOCKING LIBRARY DOORS

Have a big door shown partly open with keys attached to the keyhole and streamers going to a set of books. The idea is to show what the library can "unlock" as to information. You could also have a large safe with "Valuable Information."

WAR BATTLES

Make a display depicting a famous battle of a war and display with military history books.

TREASURE CHEST

Fill a treasure chest with ideas of what the library has to offer.

RUSSIAN NESTED DOLLS

Borrow someone's nested dolls and arrange from largest to smallest. Books could also be arranged behind or in front of the dolls or on an upper or lower shelf of corresponding sizes. Use the heading "The Library Can Find Your Information No Matter How Big or Small." Try to simulate nested books by placing a very large one on the bottom and going to a very small one on the top.

BOOKMARKER

A collection of bookmarkers was sent for and used in this display along with the books they advertised. The entire background was filled with the bookmarkers. To fill in the empty spaces in the display, items were placed in along with the books. For example, a pair of ballet shoes was placed alongside the book Ballet Shoes by Noel Streatfield. A small tiger was added with the book Tiger Eyes by Judy Blume.

FLIGHT

We purchased a book of cutout airplanes and had students assemble them. They were hung at various levels with a display of books on aircraft.

LIBRARY THEMES

A group of library rules such as "Quiet Please" were printed in various languages on our computer using the Fontrix program with its Foreign Language Fontpak. We used Arabic, Hebrew, Kiragana, Katahana, Russian, and Sanskrit. Along with each language we placed a book from that country. (National Geographic magazines were used in the display where we could not find a book on the entire country.)

PHOTOGRAPHY CONTEST

Run a photography contest and display the photos. Possible themes are shots of the library itself or of people reading anywhere at all. Arrange your photography books with the photos. If someone has a camera collection they would wish to loan, add that to the display.

WHALES

If someone has a collection of whale figurines or scrimshaw, display with the heading "A Whale of a Good Time" and any kind of books.

FOREIGN LANGUAGES

Make signs (either hand-lettered or with the Print Shop) and mount on sturdy paper. The signs should be in a foreign language and have something to do with the library, such as "Use the Library" or "Libraries Are Fun," etc. Display with items from that country/ies such flags, dolls, or borrowed objects. This could also be expanded into a contest where students must translate what the signs say.

WORLD

Get a large map of the world and make this the background. Purchase small flags of the nations (can be purchased from the United Nations). Place the flag in each country where it belongs. Either make or purchase a picture of the UN building and mount it on cardboard. Stand UN building in the center of display. Pictures of UN celebrities or news items of the day could be placed in this display. This world display could be adapted to many other features of nations such as foods, costumes, languages, etc.

PART THREE

MATERIALS AND TECHNIQUES

Information in this section will cover materials such as papers, paints, inks, and adhesives. Techniques covered will be painting, lettering, gluing, enlarging, constructing, and designing as related to library displays. The data reported here are not highly technical; no difficult building instructions or sophisticated tools are needed to perform any of the tasks discussed.

MATERIALS

PAPERS: Six basic papers were used for the displays in this book--drawing paper, craft paper, oaktag, cardboard, newspaper, and illustration board. Knowledge of papers (how and what they can be used for) is an essential part of designing display.

Buying the most expensive papers and boards is not the object here. Many of the papers used may be obtained in any department or variety store. Drawing papers may be procured from any art supply store. In fact, it would be an excellent idea to visit an art supply store just to survey the variety of papers and how they may be used. The art department in your school would also be an excellent source of small quantities of paper or information such as catalogs for art supplies.

BOARDS: Boards used for display consist of Manila tag, illustration board, and everyday cardboard. Manila tag board is the same material used for Manila file folders. This is a very durable, yet easy to manipulate, board. It is very good for cutting, rolling and scoring. Manila tag accepts most painting or drawing media and will not become saturated or soggy when using water-based inks or paints. It is also an outstanding choice for cutting shapes and making stencils, because it is easy to cut yet will hold a crisp edge, which is most important when stenciling. The tag can be purchased at most paper or office supply stores. If necessary, Manila folders may also be used.

Illustration Board. Illustration board is a much heavier board. It is manufactured in a variety of weights, sizes, and finishes. Artists find it very useful when they need to have a sturdy paperlike material to paint on. Many art stores will sell illustration board in sizes from 8" x 10" to 40" x 60", depending on the type of board needed. Illustration board has several advantages over Manila tag in that large pieces may be purchased, it is a much stronger material for constructing forms, and like the Manila tag, will accept most paints and inks. The major disadvantage is that it is much more expensive and a little more difficult to work with.

Cardboard. Cardboard is probably one of the best materials to be used

93

in displaying, especially where the creation of forms is involved. It can be painted, and any paper may be glued to it. When constructing, the cardboard itself amy be easily cut, folded, and glued. Major advantages of cardboard are its availability and price. It is available almost anywhere. An excellent source for cardboard would be any store or business throwing cardboard boxes away. For large pieces, a furniture store or plumbing business are possibilities. Many of these businesses would be more than happy to give cardboard away.

BRUSHES: Most of the brushes used for these displays were not expensive artist's brushes. There are plenty of good brushes in many sizes available at your local department or hardware store. The most important thing to consider when purchasing brushes is their intended use. Some are strictly for oil-based paints, while others are more suitable for water-based paints. The same brush should not be used for both purposes. Brushes also come in a variety of widths and bristles. Enthusiastic librarians may wish to purchase a few specialized brushes such as those used for lettering. They will enable one to paint many styles of lettering in various sizes which are invaluable in displays.

ADHESIVES: Adhesives fall into two categories--liquid, such as white glue or rubber cement, and tapes, such as clear, masking, and packaging tapes. All of the above have been used to various extents in the displays, each having advantages over the others, depending on the application. White glue, traditionally known as Elmer's, was used for a great many of the displays, primarily for gluing paper to cardboard and with construction techniques. The biggest secret to using any glue is to spread it evenly before it dries. To achieve this, use cardboard squares or a brush. Rubber cement may also be used instead of white glue, but may be slightly irritating. It dries quickly, can be rubbed off, and does not bleed through paper like white glue. Tape is the most commonly used adhesive. There are many tapes on the market that vary according to their uses and sizes. Masking tape is probably the best tape for most displays. It comes in a variety of widths from 1/2" to 4". Aside from the variety of sizes, masking tape has several advantages over the traditional clear tape in that it can be torn easily by hand, can be written on, and is relatively strong. A new item on the adhesive market is in spray form. This is quick and easy, but is also very expensive and the fumes can be irritating.

MISCELLANEOUS: There are many materials incorporated into the displays that best fit into the "miscellaneous" category. Materials such as paper clips, boxes, string, wood, plastic, styrofoam, and the like are listed and discussed with the individual displays. All materials used in the displays are common, everyday items and can be obtained locally.

SYMBOLS

Every day we see designs in the form of familiar symbols such as road signs, trademarks, and logos. Many are simplifications of realistic forms. Others are design inventions that became meaningful only through association with certain ideas, words, slogans, or products. Symbols or simplified forms are probably one of the best images for displays. Students will easily recognize a symbol they can associate with the theme of the display and there would be no need for the librarian to come up with a realistic rendering of the subject matter. An excellent example of this is the pink flamingos in the "Library Vice" display. Most people could easily associate the flamingos and the "Library Vice" sign with the popular "Miami Vice" TV program. Other examples would be the marquee in the movie display and the large heart in the Valentine display. All these designs were very simple and used familiar symbols.

PATTERNS

Design is familiar to us in the form of pattern. We discern pattern in any orderly arrangement or sequence of similar shapes. Pattern is widely used for ornamentation, as in textiles, wallpaper, architecture, etc. Pattern design in a display may be used in several ways. One is the actual placement of patterns as a border or background in the display. A shape or image may be repeated throughout. A good example of this use of pattern as background is the sheet music incorporated into the music display. Another example is the election buttons repeated as the background for the election display.

BALANCE

The logic and precision of balance helps to maintain order in displays as they do in life. However, an absence of balance can create forces that are sometimes disruptive but often interesting. You will have occasion to use both balance and imbalance in display. In display design, balance would be needed when deciding how many objects or images are to be in the display and what size these images should be. A perfect example that illustrates the use of balance is the space display. We had plenty of robots, spacemen, spaceships, and various other vehicles to use in this display. However, we wanted to balance the objects on the ground with those floating in space without covering the entire painted background area. As can be seen, a good balance was created by just hanging one spaceship in each display off-center with a small ship or vehicle to one side and even smaller objects in the foreground of the entire display. This is another instance where simplification was used. Filling the entire

95

display with as many objects as possible would have been distracting. Also, the books must be in balance with the display objects.

Another example of balance is the unicorn display, where the attempt was to have nearly the same objects on both sides of the display, almost like a mirror image.

TECHNIQUES

DESIGN: Many people seem to feel the word "design" entails a great deal of technical and artistic ability. We see designers, like artists, as people born with this great magical talent of creating fantastic pictures from nothing. Not true. The task of any designer, no matter what is being designed, is to communicate information in the clearest possible way to the audience.

The first stage in creating any design is planning. A design, in this case for a display, should be viewed as a problem that needs a solution. A series of questions should be asked: (1) Is there a general or specific theme or concept in mind? (2) Are there images available that would best fit the theme? (3) What materials would be needed for the display?

Probably the most important element of design is simplicity. Many otherwise perfect displays can be ruined by the person who feels that more is better.

Several design principles will be discussed. These should not be committed to memory and applied with inflexible pressure, like multiplication tables. But they can, and should, become part of your general approach to creating a display.

COMPOSITION: Composition is much like balance in that it deals with the location of the objects used in a display. A display, like a room, may be bare and empty, crowded and cluttered, or have too much in one corner. Under ordinary conditions, none of these extremes is good. Designing a display calls for the same kind of judgment used in solving everyday problems.

COLOR: Every person who uses color should have a clear understanding of what color is, now to organize it, and how to use it to the best advantage. Color is a highly personal and variable element.

There are, however, certain basic principles in the handling of color. To work with color, it is not necessary to study or memorize complicated color systems. The most important information needed for displays is how to mix two or more colors to achieve the one you want and how to combine different colors in pleasing and effective compositions.

Another area of importance is color symbolism or association. Certain colors immediately suggest certain moods to the average person. Each display may call for the use of different colors. One example of this is the Vietnam display. Of course, one would not want to use bright oranges, yellows, and reds that would traditionally suggest an upbeat, happy message for this display. Instead, dark, subdued greens were used to go along with the Vietnam army theme, and the gun and letters were left white to contrast with the background. Color symbolism is also present in the Valentine display, where bright reds and very colorful miniature book covers were used.

For production reasons, the displays pictured in this book are in black and white. Whenever possible, special mention is made of the colors used.

PAINTING: There are two basic painting techniques: wash and opaque painting. A wash is where the paint is applied very thinly in a transparent fashion. When using water-soluble paints such as acrylic, watercolors, tempera, or even inks, the more water used, the more transparent the paint will become. The advantage of using a wash technique is the quickness of drying time and application. A wash technique should be planned in order to avoid unwanted areas from being painted. However, opaque paint can often be used to correct mistakes made with transparent painting.

A fine example of the wash technique is the skiing display. The ski lodge was quickly painted with transparent colors. The dark lines used for the wood grain and windows were drawn in over the paint with a marker after the paint had dried. Another example is the locker display which needed a rather large area to be painted. The lockers themselves were painted with a transparent wash; the lines drawn in later with a yardstick and dark magic marker.

Many times opaque techniques are needed, especially when something must be completely covered with nothing showing through. The advantages of using the opaque technique are that it completely covers the area and changes can always be made no matter what color or shade is used. The opaque technique is also used when painting lettering because of the need to contrast the lettering with the images.

LETTERING: Lettering plays a very important role in displaying. Its primary function is to identify the theme of the display and enhance the images used. There are several lettering techniques incorporated into the displays.

Lettering can get very technical and expensive. However, almost any lettering may be easily copied or traced from any source. In the locker display, the lettering above the locker ("Check for Overdue Books") was traced and enlarged from a lettering source book. Many of the displays used plastic letters with pins in the back. These are very convenient and can be purchased at any stationery store or from school supply catalogs. They come in a variety of sizes, styles, and colors.

Plastic stick-on letters were also used, such as in the movie display. These are particularly good when the surface being used will be used again with different words. Such as on the movie marquee, it is better to be able to change the title rather than draw or paint the words directly onto the surface, which would then need to be repainted for each new title. A disadvantage of the stick-on letters is the expense incurred when purchasing several styles or sizes. This is where you could buy paper letters or make your own from paper or cardboard.

Transfer, or rub-on letters are clean and professional looking but are permanent. They also come in a wide variety of styles and sizes but can be expensive.

A favorite lettering technique is stenciling, which has come a long way. There are many new stencil techniques and lettering styles available.

If you have access to a computer, you may wish to use a program such as The Print Shop by Broderbund or other lettering programs to produce signs and banners in different styles and sizes.

CONSTRUCTION: There are several construction techniques employed when building displays. The most common and simplest is gluing cardboard together to create three-dimensional (3-D) effects. With any construction technique using papers and cardboards, the ability to manipulate the material is very important. We shall discuss several paper-manipulation techniques such as bending, tearing, curling, folding, and scoring as related to the displays in the book.

Looking at the TV display, you will see a large TV set with screen effect and controls. The television was constructed by cutting a square or rectangular hole in the cardboard to fit the opening of the display case. Of course, it can be adapted to any size case. The 3-D effect was obtained by the fact that the inside of the case was perceived as the inside of a set, further enhanced by outlining the screen and controls.

Outlining itself helps to create the 3-D effect because it shows an edge or thickness (see Figure 1).

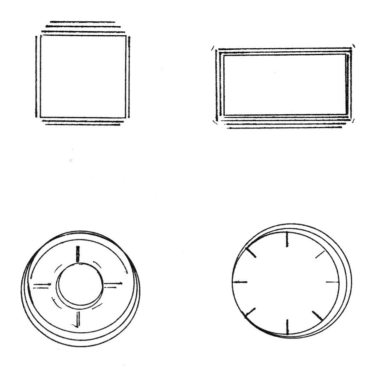

Figure 1

Another way to show three-dimensionality is with shadows. Shadows, dark and light areas, will appear on any 3-D object depending on which direction the light is coming from. This can easily be seen in the space display. Looking at the planets in the background, they appear to be spheres or 3-D balls. However, they are not. The three-dimensionality was achieved by shading the bottom of the planets dark and keeping the top light. In space, there would have to be a light source. Of course, in designing one can take liberties when deciding where the light is coming from.

Another example of a 3-D effect by using lines and shading is the peek-through fence display. The fence was drawn on a flat piece of cardboard; the lines and shadows at the top give the fence the appearance of thickness.

The "Library Vice" display is a good example of creating a 3-D effect. The leaves were cut from green construction paper and folded through the middle to create a lifelike 3-D leaf.

In the movie display, the folding technique is employed again with the marquee. However, this time a piece of cardboard was scored slightly on the same side as the fold to achieve an even crease. When folding or bending heavier materials such as cardboard, it always helps to score or cut the area to be folded. This process is only needed to break the surface enough to get the fold started. This allows more control over the fold.

The scoring, folding, and curling techniques can be seen in the Valentine display. The large heart was constructed with plain brown cardboard. Two heart shapes were first drawn on two large pieces of cardboard. To achieve the 3-D effect of thickness for the box, several pieces of paper were cut into strips two inches wide. These strips were curled by running them over scissors as when curling ribbon for wrapping gifts. The curled strips were glued to the cardboard hearts leaving an edge of about one inch around the heart. Tabs were attached to the curled strips about every two inches rather than relying only on the edge of the strips (see Figure 2).

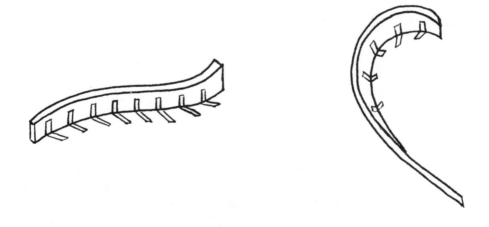

Figure 2

Remember, the primary purpose is the look of a Valentine box of candy. It is not imperative for the box to be functional as well. The entire box was painted a bright red with acrylic paint.

One of the best displays that illustrates cardboard construction techniques is the locker display. The lockers were constructed by gluing together various pieces of cardboard. These were made in three sections: one piece of cardboard measuring 1 foot by 5 feet on the left, the middle section was 3 by 5 feet folded into three 1-foot sections, and the piece on the right was a 2 by 5-feet piece (see figures 3a and 3b).

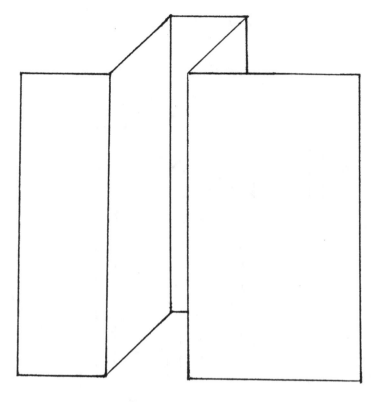

Figure 3a

Again, scoring the cardboard lightly in the middle section eases the folding. Also, tabs were used when gluing the sections together. White paper then covered the entire set of lockers, which allowed for lines to be drawn around the doors and locks for a more 3-D effect.

COPYING AND ENLARGING: There are many ways to copy and enlarge images. Here we shall concentrate on the simplest and most economical.

Tracing paper is one of the best friends to librarians designing displays. It can be used in many ways; the most common is "doubling" as inexpensive carbon paper. Tracing paper is placed over the image, which is penciled in. The tracing paper is then flipped over, and a pencil is rubbed on the back of the image, which is thereby transferred to any surface. Tracing paper has the advantage over regular carbon paper in that it allows the image being traced to be seen. This is very important, especially when tracing over several images at once or when combining parts of different images into one.

Copying and enlarging can also vary according to the type of machine used. A photocopier or xerographic machine are found in most offices. Many new machines now have enlarging options. The entire basis of our New York display was a 4" x 5" ad enlarged on a photocopier.

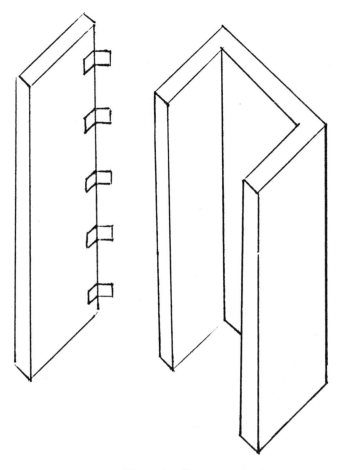

Figure 3b

(The ad was cut into six equal sections that kept being enlarged until there was enough material to cover the background of the display case. Looking closely at this display, one can see some of the same buildings repeated. This does not detract from the overall effect.) Another enlargement from the photocopier was the periodic table in the chemistry display. These machines are an invaluable tool. If there is none at your disposal, other methods of enlarging such as using an opaque or overhead projector can be employed, but are not nearly as time-saving.

There are several models of both opaque and overhead projectors. The main difference between an overhead and an opaque is the image it projects. An opaque projector will project an opaque image: magazine pictures, photographs, even real items. By moving the projector closer or further away from the wall, the image it projects can be either enlarged or reduced. A piece of paper can be taped to the wall and then traced. The disadvantage here is that opaque projectors must be used in extreme darkness.

Probably the most versatile machine is the overhead projector. Most school librarians have access to one. The overhead has several advantages when designing displays. The image, once made into a transparency (which can be done on most copiers), can be enlarged, reduced, modified, or combined in a number of ways with other images to create very interesting effects. The fact that you are working with a transparent material makes it a lot easier to adjust the image to be projected. It is also easier to combine several transparencies on one machine and project them all at once.

The map in the Christopher Columbus display was enlarged with an overhead projector, as was the gun in the Vietnam display. The lettering on the locker display, "Check for Overdue Books," was traced from a lettering book, the tracing duplicated on a copier onto a transparency, and then enlarged on an overhead projector. No matter what materials or machines are used, experimenting with them will yield many new ideas.

THINGS TO HAVE ON HAND

Old magazines	Pinup letters
Styrofoam (pieces and "peanuts")	Stencils
Mailing tubes	Paper letters
Cardboard boxes (various sizes)	Old newspapers
Maps	Food coloring
Leaves	Vases
Branches	Old filmstrips, films
Dried flowers	Crepe paper (rolls/sheets)
Sand	Markers
Stones	Hangers
Shells	Book stands
Glue	Packing straw
Tape	Rope
Construction paper	Lace
Oak tag paper	Old wooden crates
Netting	Paint brushes (various sizes)
Straight pins	Wood blocks
Tacks	Coffee cans
Thread	Sign holders
String	Plastic picture frames
Paint (spray, poster, etc.)	Posters
Cloth (various colors, textures)	Photocopier
Wooden dowels	Overhead projector

SOURCES

ALA
Public Information Office
50 East Huron Street
Chicago, IL 60611

A source of display and promotional materials for libraries.

Belleprohon Books
36 Anacapa Street
Santa Barbara, CA 93101

A catalog of coloring books, cut-and-assemble books, and paper dolls.

Book Report
Linworth Publishers, Inc.
P.O. Box 14466
Columbus, OH 43214

A periodical full of ideas for the library.

Children's Book Council
67 Irving Place
New York, NY 10003

A great source for free and inexpensive materials such as posters, book-marks, pamphlets, author/illustrator brochures, and such.

Dover Publications, Inc.
31 East Second Street
Mineola, NY 11501

A catalog of high-quality and inexpensive books in every field of interest. Also posters, paper-doll books, stickers, cut-and-use stencils, cut-and-assemble toy books, and much more.

Dynamic Graphics, Inc.
6000 North Forest Park Drive
P.O. Box 1901
Peoria, IL 61656-1901

A catalog of art services and supplies along with references to help you do your displays or bulletin boards much faster and more creatively.

Library Educational Institute, Inc.
R.D. #1, P.O. Box 219
New Albany, PA 18833

Books on displays, graphic design, promotional and clip art, printing, publicity, and more.

National Gallery of Art
Sixth St. & Constitution Ave., NW
Washington, DC 20565

A great source for purchasing prints and pictures.

Paper Models International
9910 SW Bonnie Brae Drive
Beaverton, OR 97005

A beautiful collection of card models of buildings, cars, aircraft, birds, dinosaurs, etc.

ST Publications
407 Gilbert Street
Cincinnati, OH 45202

Books on lettering and craft techniques, merchandising, visual design, sign design.

Step-by-Step Graphics
6000 North Forest Park Drive
P.O. Box 1901
Peoria, IL 61656-1901

A how-to reference magazine for visual communication.

Upstart
P.O. Box 889
Hagerstown, MD 21741

A catalog of library promotional materials such as bookmarks, posters, bulletin board decorations, balloons, book bags, mobiles, etc.

INDEX